HOPE FOR THE HOPELESS

*Finding Hope
One Page at a Time*

31 DAY DEVOTIONAL

Myrtle H. Greene

HOPE FOR THE HOPELESS
Copyright © 2005 Myrtle H. Greene

All Rights Reserved

ISBN: 1-59352-146-4

Published by:
Christian Services Network
1975 Janich Ranch Ct.
El Cajon, CA 92019
Toll Free: 1-866-484-6184
www.CSNbooks.com

Contact Author at:
Myrtle H. Greene
P.O. Box 350412
Jacksonville, Florida 32235
904-642-9294

No part of this publication may be reproduced, stored in a retrieval system, or transmitted in any way by any means - electronic, mechanical, photocopy, recording, or otherwise, without the prior permission of the copyright holder, except as provided by USA copyright law.

Printed in the United States of America.

Dedication

This book is dedicated first and foremost to Almighty God for entrusting me to write words of hope for his people. I consider it an honor to "pen" God's message that there is hope in any situation. Thank you Heavenly Father for the gift!

To my best friend and main supporter who has been my biggest fan for over 23 years, my husband, James. Without your support I could have not completed this book. Your love and prayers carried me through to the other side. Thank you for allowing me to be all God has placed inside of me!

Also to my precious sons, James Jr. and Johnathan. You both caused me to go on in my darkest hours. Thanks for supporting "mommy" in this writing process.

To my pastor, Bishop Paul Zink of New Life Christian Fellowship for the message, Discipline and Obedience leads to Responsibility. This message motivated me to complete this book. Also to my church cell group "family", thanks for the prayers and encouragement. Your support has been a blessing to me throughout the years.

Last of all, to my family and friends for walking with me through this vision until completion. God always knows the right people to place in your life to accomplish His purpose.

In Loving Memory

In loving memory of some special people who touched my life forever and inspired me to write. My daughter, Jessica she taught me to love others and myself unconditionally. Also my daughter, Jamilia everytime I looked into her sparkling eyes I saw hope! To Debra Mincey, God hand picked her to be my best friend that taught me to "dance" no matter what.

Table of Contents

Dedication iii
In Loving Memory v

Day 1 11
  Storms Don't Last Forever
Day 2 13
  Refuse to Die
Day 3 15
  Today I Cried
Day 4 17
  In the Midst
Day 5 19
  Troubles Won't Have the Last Word
Day 6 21
  Change Your Expectations
Day 7 23
  Strong Versus Strength
Day 8 25
  A Diamond in the Rough
Day 9 27
  Nothing Just Happens

Day 10 29
    It's a Good Thing
Day 11 31
    Dead, But Still Alive
Day 12 33
    Ain't Nothing Like the Real Thing
Day 13 35
    Providence of God
Day 14 37
    Come to the Table
Day 15 39
    Freedom Comes With a Price
Day 16 41
    Reassess "Your" Situation
Day 17 43
    "Flashbacks"
Day 18 45
    Do Yourself
Day 19 47
    Keep the Mask Off
Day 20 49
    Empty the Trash
Day 21 51
    The Value of Valleys
Day 22 53
    Don't Look Back, Don't Go Back
Day 23 55
    Pick Yourself Up!!!

DAY 24 57
  Be Careful
DAY 25 59
  Jesus Is...
DAY 26 61
  Finish the Furnace
DAY 27 63
  Hear and Obey
DAY 28 65
  Don't Just Survive, but Thrive
DAY 29 67
  Stop, Drop, and Go
DAY 30 69
  Follow "Your" Peace
DAY 31 71
  He is Still God!
ABOUT THE AUTHOR 73

x

Day 1

Storms Don't Last Forever

John 16:33 (AMP):

I have told you these things, so that in Me you may have peace and confidence. In the world you have tribulation and trials and distress and frustration; but be of good cheer! For I have overcome the world. (I have deprived it of power to harm you and have conquered it for you.

The one thing that we are guaranteed in life is to have "storms," according to John 16:33. In that same Scripture we can rejoice because it says that Jesus has already overcome them for you.

When you are in your storm of a broken relationship, a storm of temptation, or a financial storm, know that this too shall pass. On a recent trip, I began driving and ran into a storm. I stayed in the storm until I almost reached my destination. All of a sudden the winds calmed, the rain ceased, and I saw the sun again! So it is with your storm, just keep on going and remember that nothing on earth lasts forever...it just seems to! Tell yourself...this too shall pass! The hurt will pass, the confusion will pass, and the disappointment will pass. Look for your sun in the "Son" because it's right up the road!

DAY 2

REFUSE TO DIE

Psalm 119:17 (AMP):

I shall not die but live, and shall declare works and recount the illustrious acts of the Lord.

Don't you dare tell yourself this is the end...and that you will never feel better again! That is a lie straight from Satan himself, so don't believe it! Remember that God makes everything beautiful in his time (Ecc 3:11). He will make your heart whole again and that pain will get less until it's gone. You have to "refuse" to die and "decide" to live, and all of heaven will back you up.

When my 5 month old baby died of crib death I thought I would die too. I had to make a decision to LIVE and TRUST God that I would make it through. Sometimes I had to decide this two and three times a day until the pain lessened in my heart. So confess today...I will live and not die, and declare the works of God in my situation. See your hurt as a hurdle, jump over it, and keep running to the finish line! Refuse to die until you win!

Day 3

Today I Cried

Psalm 30:5b (AMP):

Weeping may endure for a night, but joy comes in the morning.

Tears are a sign that you are human, and not a sign of weakness. Remember, when Jesus heard that Lazarus was dead, He wept.

When you have experienced loss of any kind, to weep is a "natural" response. But to have joy after the weeping is a "supernatural" response that God does when we trust Him. Just remember it is ok to cry! God sees your tears, bottles them up, and causes your enemies to turn back (Psalms 56:8-9). So, the next time you feel like crying, go ahead and let it flow. While you are crying, remember the precious promises for your tears. Just imagine that every time you cry your tears are falling into a "bottle of expectancy" that only God can fulfill in His time.

DAY 4

In the Midst

Psalm 46:5 (AMP):

God is in the midst of her, she shall not be moved; God will help her right early (at the dawn of the morning).

If you can find PEACE	IN THE MIDST
If you can find QUIETNESS	IN THE MIDST
If you can find HOPE	IN THE MIDST
If you can keep your FOCUS	IN THE MIDST

I believe you have found the true meaning of life and that is to Live, no matter what, LIVE! Nothing can separate you from the love of God (Romans 8:35), even when you are in the middle of a fiery trial.

Even when God seems distant and your trials seem closer, you can still have peace, quietness, hope, and keep your focus. David complained about God delaying in helping him (Psalm 13:1), but at the end he rejoiced for God blessing him. Remember that it takes more faith to go through a trial than to go around it.

DAY 5

Troubles Won't Have the Last Word

Psalm 91:15:

He shall call upon Me, and I will answer him; I will be with him trouble, I will deliver him and honor him.

When I was a young girl, I would hear my mother say, "Troubles won't last always." I didn't quite understand that phrase, but somehow it brought me comfort that God was really in control, and not the trouble. How do we outlast our troubles? We can take three courses of action: Pray, Praise, and Trust. We should always pray and ask God's presence into every situation in our lives (Philipians 4:6). Praise God that He is greater than our troubles and has already made a way for us. Sometimes to praise God is a sacrifice when all is not well, but it will help you. Finally, we must trust God. Trusting God means entering into His rest while the troubles are there. These courses of action should not be optional in our lives, but done habitually until the troubles cease and the victory is ours!

DAY 6

Change Your Expectations

Proverbs 23:18 (AMP):

For surely there is a latter end (a future and a reward) and your hope and expectation shall be not cut off.

To expect is to look forward to or to anticipate change in a situation. Do you "expect" your situation to change? Do you expect your heart will ever heal? Or have you simply given up and decided this is the way I will end up? Whether you were an innocent bystander or the main cause of your situation, you can still expect God to bring something good out of it. The Bible's promise is that all things work together for the good for those that love God and are called according to his purpose (Rom. 8:28). "All" includes the good, the bad, and the ugly things we encounter. Faith in God's Word fuels your expectation to see a miracle in your trial. Remember, where you are doesn't have to be where you end if you "expect" change!

Day 7

Strong Versus Strength

Philippians 4:13:

I have the strength for all things in Christ Who empowers me. I am ready for anything and equal to anything through Him Who infuses inner strength into me; I am self-sufficient in Christ's sufficiency.

Even though I have always considered myself as a strong person, that alone has not been sufficient in going through hopeless situations. As if you haven't already figured this out or come to the place that life will hand you some things you can't handle! No matter how "strong" you think you are physically, emotionally, or even spiritually (you super saint!). Being "strong" will not pull you out victoriously but the "strength" that comes from God will. With the strength from God you will be ready for anything and equal to anything (Philippians 4:13). So quickly run out of yourself and remember a "strong" woman has faith that she is strong enough for the battles. But a woman of "strength" has faith that through her battles God will strengthen her.

Day 8

A Diamond in the Rough

Job 23:10 (AMP):

But He knows the way that I should take. When He has tried me, I shall come forth as refined gold.

It was once said that diamonds are a girl's best friend. Oh, how we love to marvel at the beauty of a diamond that has been perfected and polished to excellence. Not for a moment do we consider the process which this diamond has been through to shine so brightly. Diamonds have great power to reflect light. But to produce the greatest possible brilliance, a diamond must be cut, polished, and shaped exactly to perfection. You are a diamond in the rough places of life. If you would allow God to "cut" your fleshly way of doing things, then He can polish you with His anointing and shape you into the diamond that would reflect His light. Remember, the rough place you are in will pass, and then you will shine like a diamond!

DAY 9

Nothing Just Happens

Proverbs 16: 33 (AMP):

The lot is cast into the lap, but the decision is wholly of the Lord (even the events that seem accidental are really ordered by Him.)

A good man's or woman's steps are ordered by the Lord (Psalms 37:23). A circumstance is never an "happenstance," but a part of your destiny. Even the trial you just came through or maybe are still in didn't just happen. We are not delivered from trials when we become saved, but we are given power to overcome them. So, quit worrying about how and why this thing happened in your life. Begin to confess who you are in Christ, and that He is control! As you grow and become more yielded, only then can God fully display His glory through you. Realize that He is the God of the happenstance in our lives. Remember Ruth and how she was led to the right field with the right owner, Boaz. She was being led by God and didn't even know it. Could you be standing in your field of opportunity and it doesn't look like you think it should? Look again at where God has allowed you to be...and find the grains of blessing he has purposely left for you!

Day 10

It's a Good Thing

Psalms 119:71:

It is good for me that I have been afflicted, that I might learn Your statutes.

I realize that when you are going through a tough time you are less likely to say this that is a "good thing." But how else will you get to know God and his faithfulness toward you if not for the tough times?

I have to admit this has not always been easy for me to say, especially in my earlier Christian walk. After walking through so many valleys and watching God bring me back every time to the mountain top, my spiritual eyes were opened! I began to realize how I was growing and maturing in Christ after each valley.

Trust me, when you come out of this tough time, just look back for a moment. You will see the faithfulness of God in your life and your heart will rejoice. The joy of your salvation will far outweigh the tough time that tried to hinder you. Furthermore, you will be able to say,

"I never thought I would know God like this for myself." Even when we give out and feel like giving up, God never breaks His covenant of love toward us. When this revelation becomes a reality there will be absolutely nothing the devil can do to stop you! So, look at the benefits of the tough times and not the trials!

DAY 11

Dead, But Still Alive

Job 14:14 (AMP):

If a man dies, shall he live again? All the days of my warfare and service I will wait, till my change and release come.

Job asked, "If a man dies, shall he live again?" Can you actually go through so much that you feel dead on the inside? Your life can be so full of warfare that going through the motions becomes a way of life.

No one knows this is true better than I do. I did not recognize the warning signs in my life until I felt completely dead on the inside. I felt my hope fading and I really could not explain to anyone what I was experiencing. The Spirit of the Lord comforted me by letting me know I was going through a "winter" season and it would pass. I began to study the winter season in the natural to better understand what I was going through. In the winter everything looks dead (grass, flowers, etc...), but the roots are still alive and well. So it was with me, my emotions may have felt dead but my spirit (root of my existence) was alive!

So don't over-react to your winter season but wait till your change and release comes like Job. He was confident that he would not die in his trials, but he would live again. Guess what? God turned Job's captivity and restored his fortunes greater than he had before. God is no respecter of persons, so hold on and tell God, "I wont let go until you bless me."

Day 12

Ain't Nothing Like the Real Thing

Genesis 18:14:

Is there any thing too hard for the Lord? At the time appointed I will return unto thee, according to the time of life, and Sarah shall have a son.

Substitution brings destitution, because nothing takes the place of what God has purposed for your life. Whatever God promised that He will do in your life is always worth waiting for. Sarah got impatient and encouraged Abraham to have a child with Hagar. She settled for a substitute and eventually this led to destitution of her relationship with Hagar, Ishmael, and Abraham. Most of all, Sarah brought destitution to her relationship with God by not trusting Him to bring the promise of a child to pass.

How many times do we substitute and give birth to an Ishmael instead of birthing our promise an Isaac? When we allow patience to have her perfect work in us we always get the real thing. It is always a temptation when we are feeling hopeless and want a quick fix. Resist that temptation to medicate your pain and wait on God for the healing. Remember God's ways are not like our ways and His timing is always on time (Habakkuk 2:3).

Day 13

Providence of God

Psalm 139:16 (AMP):

Your eyes saw my unformed substance, and in Your book all the days (of my life) were written before ever they took shape, when as yet there was none of them.

Even though your life may seem to be in "chaos" from the trial you are in, or have faced in the past, there is still hope. That hope lies in the providence or divine guidance of God toward you. In easier terms, God is still God and He is in control of your destiny. Your mistakes, failures, or bad choices do not change the plan God has for you. It is still yours if you still want it, believe it, and wait until it comes to past. No thing or no one can change God's divine guidance for you. You are the clay and God is the Potter. He is shaping you into what you were designed to be and do on this earth. So remember when you are surrounded by troubles, God will preserve you against the anger of your enemies (Palms 32:7), and work out His plans for your life (Jeremiah 29:11).

Day 14

Come to the Table

Psalm 23:5 (AMP):

You prepare a table before me in the presence of my enemies.

God prepares a table for you in the presence of your enemies. What are your enemies? A broken relationship that gave you a broken heart, or broken finances with no hope in sight. Whatever the situation is you qualify to come to the table of the Lord and eat. On the table you will find living water that quenches your thirst forever. Also the bread of life that satisfies the hunger you have been trying to fill through other means. All you have to do is to stop eating the crumbs off the floor and sit at the table and feast. Tell yourself, "No more crumbs," only the best from the King's table will I accept. You do not have to settle any more because through Christ you can have life and its abundance. So pull out your chair, get your napkin, and enjoy the meal of life that God has prepared for you.

Day 15

Freedom Comes With a Price

Galatians 5:1 (AMP):

In this freedom Christ has made us free (and completely liberated us); stand fast then, and do not be hampered and ensnared and submit to a yoke of slavery (once you have put it off).

When you go into a department store you see price tags on the items for sale. Even the overstocked, outdated, and clearance items still have a price tag on them. My husband often says, "Salvation is free, but the anointing costs you." Jesus Christ has paid the ultimate price, but you and I have to do something to receive what belongs to us.

Your "freedom" from the trial you are facing comes with a price. You need the anointing of the Holy Spirit to help you resist the world's way of going through seemingly hopeless situations. Easier said than done, even for the mature Christian not to be conformed to the world's way. This type of freedom begins with renewing your mind in the Word of God (Romans 12:2). Find out what is the good and acceptable and perfect will of God for you in this situation. Sometimes your freedom may come with the price of walking away from the familiar and stepping into unknown territory. It may be severing relationships that are draining you of your vision. I call those "high maintenance" relationships, with expensive price tags attached. If you want it badly enough, no price will be too expensive to live free!

Day 16

Reassess "Your" Situation

Matthew 7:3 (AMP):

Why do you stare from without at the very small particle that is in your brother's eye but do not become aware of the beam of timber that is in your own eye?

The key to really finding hope again and keeping that hope alive is to reassess "your" situation while in the situation. The key word is "your," not whomever you believe is the person at fault. Your situation may be primarily caused by someone else's decision, but you can only reassess your part. You bring "you" to the feet of Jesus and receive what you need for yourself. Judging your own self, so you do not have to judged, is a quick way to move from being hopeless to hoping again. Allowing God to show you yourself can be a defining moment in your life. (Warning Label: It can get ugly). Looking at yourself as the Spirit reveals from the inside out will be life-changing, with earthly benefits and eternal rewards.

When I am in a seemingly hopeless place I always ask God to show me myself. So even if my situation doesn't change right away God always changes me to be more like Him in that hopeless place.

DAY 17

"Flashbacks"

Philippians 3:13 (AMP):

I do not consider brethren, that I have captured and made it my own (yet): but one thing I do (it is my one aspiration): forgetting what lies behind and straining forward to what lies ahead.

You are on the road to recovery! You are feeling better and stronger every day. You even feel like getting your praise on again! The feeling of hopelessness is less and less. You can finally see the sun again in the midst of the clouds. You are even looking better and your smile has returned and then...

All of a sudden you hear a familiar song or a phrase that makes you remember the hole you just crawled out of. You even begin to feel the emotions again that were attached to that hopeless situation. It is as if someone hit the rewind button in your mind. I call these "flashbacks," for what is behind you suddenly forges ahead in your mind. What do you do when this happens? Quickly hit the fast forward button in your mind and don't get sucked back into that hole of despair. You do not have to participate in the flashbacks, because you can cast them down (2 Corinthians 10:5). The battle is in your mind, and you can stop it there and move on!

Day 18

Do Yourself

Matthew 22:39 (AMP):

You shall love your neighbor as (you do) yourself.

One of the golden rules you probably learned as a child was, *"Do unto others as you would have them do unto you."* Also, you might have learned the Scripture that it is better to give than to receive.

All the above is true and should be a part of our lives daily. But I believe you can hit such a bump in the road that if you don't learn to put yourself on your "to do" list there will be no more you! To do yourself, in simpler terms, is to make yourself a priority, because God does. You have been through multiple battles and you are feeling hopeless and "beat down." It is time to pull away with just you and God. My close friends laughed at me when I first told them I was taking a day off from my normal routine to spend time with myself and God. Even my family thought the idea was a bit extreme, but I knew I needed to "do myself" for a day. You need a time of refreshing for what some call a retreat, or a sabbatical, and afterwards "do yourself" in the natural. We often neglect our needs, so pamper yourself with some much-needed rest, or a spa appointment, and find a reason to laugh! If you do these often there will be a better you and more of you "to do" for others.

Day 19

Keep the Mask Off

Matthew 6:17 (AMP):

But when you fast, perfume your head and wash your face.

I attended a women's retreat that taught me a lesson about keeping the mask off. A beauty consultant took us through a step-by-step cleansing process for our faces. She gave us some cream to put on our faces and left it on for a few minutes. This was a deep cleansing mask that was supposed to clean the inner layers of our skin, but it had to be removed eventually. Although it served a good purpose, it was not to be worn all the time. She warned us about wearing a mask (fake smile) on the outside when we were totally messed up on the inside. Sometimes when we have been through so many hopeless battles we are tempted to put on our "I'm ok" mask. We do not want others to know just how broken we are on the inside so we pretend to have it all together. If you really want to go from hopelessness to hope, it again starts from the inside out. A mask may hide us from others, but not from God. So do as the Scripture says when you fast or are going through something, wash your face or keep it real. When my 12-year-old special-needs daughter died from pneumonia I could have put on an "I'm o.k. mask." But I had family and friends that encouraged me to be real. I was angry, hurt, and highly disappointed that she did not make it through yet another illness. Without the mask, my hope for life was restored and so will yours! I'm a witness!

Day 20

Empty the Trash

James 1:21 (AMP):

Wherefore lay apart all filthiness and superfluity (overflowing) of naughtiness (wickedness), and receive with meekness the engrafted word, which is able to save your souls.

My eleven-year-old son has a habit of cleaning his room and leaving his trash can full. I would constantly tell him that his room was not completely clean until the trash was emptied. One day he failed again to follow instructions and his whole room had a foul odor. My son had thrown his food away (grilled salmon) that he chose not to eat three days ago.

What trash are you allowing to stay inside of you that is causing a foul odor, instead of you being a sweet-smelling savour for Christ (Ephesians 5:2)? Letting go of all the trash of bitterness, indignation, bad temper, and resentment could be your key to victory! Sometimes injustices done to us can create deep hurts and wounds in our spirit and be manifested through our behavior. Learning to empty out all those negative feelings and trusting God leads us to hope again. He is the one who binds up and heals your broken heart. So don't let the trash of the world stay inside of you, but take out the trash of your heart daily.

DAY 21

The Value of Valleys

Psalms 23:4 (AMP):

Yes, though I walk through the (deep, sunless) valley of the shadow of death, I will fear no evil, for you are with me; Your rod (to protect) and your staff (to guide), they comfort me.

I grew up singing a song in the church choir: "He is the lily of the valley and a bright morning star." I did not realize the valleys that were ahead for me when I became a young woman and on my own. I really believed if I did all the "right" things that God would allow me to skip the valleys. I soon learned that not only would I go through the valleys, but I needed to recognize the value of them.

A valley is defined as a low point or condition. Whatever valley you are going through, I guarantee you there is some value for you to gain from it. Ask God to show you the value that is to be gained from walking through this deep and sunless place. David declared that he would fear no evil from the shadow of death. Whatever shadow of death you are facing, remember it is only a shadow and it will pass. But while you are in it look for the value. What you learn could be the bridge you build to walk out of your hopeless situation today! As my son says all the time, "You better recognize!"

DAY 22

Don't Look Back, Don't Go Back

Genesis 19:26:

But his wife looked back from behind him, and she became a pillar of salt.

For a while now you have been regaining the ground of "hope" in your life. Every day you feel stronger and the past issues are getting dimmer and dimmer in your memory. Beware of the bumps and potholes in the road you can't see. They can be a temptation to look back and even go back to what caused the situation in your life. Lot's wife looked back while going forward with her husband to the mountain and it cost her life. Jesus told his disciples that no man, having put his hand to the plough, and looking back, is fit for the kingdom of God (Luke 9:62). So declare that your storm is over and your hope is restored. No more looking back because God has promised to do a new thing by making a way in your desert and streams in your wasteland (Isa. 43:19). All of this comes from going forward consistently and not looking back or going back to the old. You might ask yourself, "How will God ever bring anything new and good out of my situation?" We cannot always understand God with our mind, but we must trust Him with our heart. So, make a decision to go forward and not backward, even in our thoughts, because it could cost you everything. Remember Lot's wife.

DAY 23

Pick Yourself Up!!!

Proverbs 24:16 (AMP):

For a righteous man falls seven times and rises again.

Ecclesiastes 3:3 says there is a time to tear down and there is a time to "build up"! Situations in the past have left you feeling torn down, but this is your season now to pick yourself up. God has promised to make everything beautiful in its time (Ecclesiastes 3:11). Believe that this is your time to come full circle with that hopeless situation. You are done with the drama of it all and you can see the sun again. The dark clouds of confusion have rolled back and you can finally put a period at the end of this trial. God's voice is so clear to you again and you look forward to communicating with Him daily. The crooked ways are becoming straight and it is time to pick up and get up, all at the same time! No more mental reasoning, because you are feeding your spirit with the Word of God. You know where you have been and the path you are now on. It is the path of life that leads upward from the "grave of troubles" (Proverbs 5:24). The final verdict is in, and you win, so PICK YOURSELF UP!

Day 24

Be Careful

Titus 3:8 (AMP):

This is a faithful saying, and these things I will that thou affirm constantly (confidently), that they which have believed God might be careful to maintain good works. These things are good and profitable.

Sometimes hopeless situations are a result of our own negligence in maintaining good works. When we are not sensitive to the Holy Spirit's leadings and promptings, we can be easily led astray.

My youngest son was watching a Saturday morning cartoon and the song got my attention. The words of the song could be helpful to children and adults for a lifetime if acted upon. The three main lines of the song were:

1. Be careful little eyes what you see.

The lust of the eye has gotten plenty of people in trouble. Make a covenant with your eyes (Job 31:1) as to what you will focus on. Also, ask God to develop your spiritual eyes so you will be able to discern right from wrong.

2. Be careful little ears what you ear.

Hearing an evil report can render you hopeless if you do not do what God's Word says about your situation. Faith is the evidence of things hoped for and faith comes by hearing the Word of God.

3. Be careful little feet where you go.

God has promised to keep your feet from falling (Psalms 116:8) if you walk with Him. Don't be led astray by your own desires and walk into the path of the enemy.

God is vitally interested in what we see, hear and where you go. He knows that the lust of the eye, the lust of the flesh, and the pride of life (1 Peter 2:11) will send us right into a hopeless situation so BE CAREFUL!

Day 25

Jesus Is...

...ALMIGHTY GOD
...WISDOM
...DELIVERER
...LION OF THE TRIBE OF JUDAH
...WORD OF LIFE
...ADVOCATE
...PROVIDER
...THE GREAT I AM
...HELPER
...SAVIOR
...PRINCE OF PEACE
...COUNSELOR
...ALPHA AND OMEGA
...FAITHFUL AND TRUE
...FORERUNNER

All of these names represent who Jesus is and will be for you in any hopeless situation. When you are going through tough times, take out your list and remind yourself what Jesus will do for you if you believe. I would constantly meditate on these names when I returned to college to complete my degree while being a mother, wife, business owner, full time employee and active church member!

I experienced Jesus being every one of those names on the list while I walked through what seem like a hopeless situation in getting my degree. I finally did graduate with my degree and I still was able to maintain all my other roles. Surely that was Jesus manifesting himself for me to wear all those hats at one time! Remember who JESUS IS...not you or me.

DAY 26

Finish the Furnace

Isaiah 48:10 (AMP):

Behold, I have refined you, but not as silver; I have tried and chosen you in the furnace of affliction.

A furnace is for gold (Proverbs 17:3), and after the fire you shall come forth as pure gold. But you must finish the furnace you are in because God chooses us for His use there. You are never alone in the furnace; just remember the fourth person who was with the Hebrew boys. The scripture says the fourth is like the Son of God, and they suffered no hurt (Daniel 3:6). What an awesome promise you and I have when we go through our fiery furnace. So whereever you are in the furnace, just keep going until you finish. Hang your feelings on a hanger and live out of a heart that trusts God. Do not worry about how hot the trials are, because the heat helps to purify you. After the furnace you will be fit for the master's use. It doesn't matter where or how you start, it's where you finish that matters.

Hope for the Hopeless

DAY 27

Hear and Obey

John 10:3b (AMP):

And the sheep listen to his voice and heed it.

Sometimes we as believers can make our lives so difficult and confusing while pursuing the will of God. You and I both have been given the power to change hopeless situations to hopeful through hearing and obeying God.

Two steps lead us right into the perfect will of God:

1) hear, and
2) obey.

Nothing more and nothing less! We make it difficult when we seek counsel in ungodly places instead of following the voice of God. When my husband and I went through tough times in our marriage I followed the voice of God, and not man. If I had not recognized God's voice and obeyed it we would have ended up in divorce court. Instead, our marriage is strong and healthy after 22 years of being together.

Your responsibility after salvation is to live your life from the inside out. No more being driven by outside influences, but now you are to be led by the Holy Spirit. Psalms 25 says when we obey Him, every path He guides us on is fragrant with His loving kindness and His truth. Now that you are at the end of your troubles, practice hearing the voice of God through His Word and prayer. The blessings will overtake you and protect you through any hopeless situation.

Day 28

Don't Just Survive, but Thrive

John 10:10 (AMP):

The thief comes in only to steal and kill and destroy, I came that they may have and enjoy life, and have it in abundance (to the full, till it overflows).

God never intended for you to crawl across the finish line of life with a testimony of survival only. He wanted you to survive and thrive according to John 10:10. How can we thrive after surviving a hopeless situation? We began to thrive by sowing into other people's lives by showing them how to come out of their situations. As freely as you have received you must give to others (Matthew 10:8). Tell others your testimony of how God brought you out when you had no hope left. God wants you to begin to declare to others that God is able and willing to help, save, and deliver them if they trust Him. We thrive when our lives help snatch our brother or sister in

Christ from the fiery trial and show them how to thrive. So rejoice that you came through some circumstances in your life and you are now ready to walk into your blood-bought destiny.

Day 29

Stop, Drop, and Go

1 Peter 5:7:

Casting the whole of your care (all your anxieties, all your worries, all your concerns, once and for all) on Him, for He cares for you affectionately and cares about you watchfully.

Methods or formulas only work if you use them consistently and in faith. One formula that I practiced to let go of things has proven successful in my life: Stop, Drop, and Go!

Stop struggling to make things happen. Stop trying to convince others who you are. Stop attempting to get God to do things for you before its time. Just Stop and Drop all your cares and concerns at the feet of Jesus. Don't be tempted to pick them up again, but GO on about doing God's business. Trust God that He will deal with your enemy (Psalms 18:17) and rescue you.

Therefore, when you become so distracted and dismayed by the circumstances and people, just remember that God has the ability to handle things in His own way and in His own time. So Stop, Drop, and Go on to the victory that lies ahead of you!

Day 30

Follow "Your" Peace

Colossians 3:15 (AMP):

And let the peace (soul harmony which comes) from Christ rule (act as umpire continually) in your hearts (deciding and settling with finality all question that arise in the minds, in that peaceful state) to which as (members of Christ's) one body you were also (to live).

When I heard a preacher quote Colossians 3:15 earlier in my Christian walk it was my "lifesaver." Up until then I never quite knew how to follow God's plan for my life. I stayed in a constant state of confusion of not knowing what to do with my life. I never knew that because the Spirit of God was in me, that I could follow my peace or inward witness. This revelation set me free from following other people's advice and opinions. I learned not to go anywhere or do anything without the peace of God, no matter how good it looked or sound. A good example was when I bought my first car without the natural knowledge of car buying. I was about to sign the contract but I felt grieved on the inside, instead of peaceful. I left that car dealership and went back to the place I had peace about and God blessed me with a car that lasted me for many years!

In any hopeless situation you may find yourself in, following the inward witness of peace will "always" bring you victory. Following your peace is like plugging into your power source. Remember the slogan.....No Jesus...No Peace....but Know Jesus....Know Peace! Follow it to victory every time!

DAY 31

He is Still God!

Hebrews 13:8 (AMP):

Jesus Christ (the Messiah) is (always) the same, yesterday, today, (yes) and forever (to the ages).

From day one of this devotional I told you that storms don't last forever. Well, what if they did? Would that change who God is or what He has promised you? Would that make God a liar? No! (Numbers 23:19) Could you trust God if the hopeless situation or storms keep on raging with no end in sight? What if the end results are different from what you were believing for? What if a loved one dies that you were believing God to heal? What if you needed a financial breakthrough and you ended up filing bankruptcy?

Does that change who God is? Each page of this journal was to help you find hope again in hopeless situations and I hope it did. But the most significant truth I hope you grasp from these 31 days is...NO MATTER WHAT COMES OR GOES IN YOUR LIFE...HE IS STILL GOD! Job lost everything but he said, "Though he slay me, yet will I trust him." In my "Job experiences of burying 2 children prematurely, marital problems, and financial crises I too learn to trust God because He still loves us, He never leaves us, His Word still stands, and He doesn't change because of our circumstances. So the next time you get a negative report or tragedy strikes, just say to yourself... HE IS STILL GOD even in this hopeless situation!

About the Author

Myrtle H. Greene is a devoted wife, proud mother of two boys, church cell group leader, women's prison volunteer and women's home fellowship leader who is passionate about helping people change their lives from the inside out. Her desire is to teach the Word of God in a way that leaves women encouraged and hungry for more of God. Myrtle's own Christian upbringing on a farm in rural North Carolina and a military background laid the foundation of tenacity and endurance that has helped her to never give up, no matter what. Her own stories included in the daily devotionals will inspire anyone to believe that all things are possible through Christ. Myrtle's life story was chosen and featured on a national television program called "Life Moments." She and her husband, James, are active in their local church as cell group pastors.